CHARRO
The Mexican Cowboy

GEORGE ANCONA

HARCOURT BRACE & COMPANY   San Diego   New York   London

The Mexican *charreada,* like our rodeo, grew out of the old methods of managing cattle on vast ranges. Today both sports celebrate their own national traditions. There are similarities between the two, but each has its own rules and sometimes violent ways of handling cattle and horses.

Gracias.

My thanks to the people who helped make this book: Rafael (La Menus) Ramírez Michel, don Pablo Barba y Barba, Gustavo Moreno S. and Ana María (La Prieta) Zermeño, Ricardo Zermeño, Hernán Díaz Batista, Ana Guadalupe Lara Díaz, Oscar Valadez Cázares, Manuel Ramírez Martínez, Rogelio Ramírez Martínez, Genoveva Rosales López, Manuel Ramos Medina of El Centro de Estudios de Historia de México Condumex, and to Marina Ancona, my daughter, who helped me with the photography.

Illustration Acknowledgments
"El vaquero echando el lazo" (the cowboy tosses his lasso) by Moritz Rugendas, lithograph by G. M. Kurz: From *México: Paisajes y bosquejos populares* by Carl Christian Sartorius. Translated into English by Mercedes Quijano Narezo from the 1859 Spanish edition of *México y los Mexicanos,* with illustrations by Moritz Rugendas; volume XXVI, second printing of the 1987 Mexican edition, CEHM CONDUMEX, Mexico, 1991.
"El ranchero" (the rancher) by Hesiquio Iriarte, lithograph by M. Murguia y Ca.: From *Los mexicanos pintados por sí mismos* by Juan de Dios Arias and others. Illustrations by engravers Hesiquio Iriarte and Andrés Campillo, colored by Emilio Tamés; new edition from 1854, volume XVI, reprint of the 1988 Mexican edition, CEHM CONDUMEX, Mexico, 1989.

Library of Congress Cataloging-in-Publication Data
Ancona, George.
Charro: the Mexican cowboy/George Ancona.
p. cm.
Summary: Text and photographs present the traditions and the annual celebration of the charro, the Mexican cowboy.
ISBN 0-15-201047-5   ISBN 0-15-201046-7 (pb)
1. Mexico—Social life and customs—Juvenile literature. 2. Charros—Mexico—Social life and customs—Juvenile literature. [1. Charros. 2. Cowboys. 3. Mexico—Social life and customs.] I. Title.
F1210.A747 1999
972—dc21   98-13396

Text set in Cochin
Designed by George Ancona and Camilla Filancia
First edition
F E D C B A   F E D C B A (pb)

Printed in Singapore

To don Pablo Barba y Barba, *charro*

Don Pablo

Don Pablo is a rancher who lives in the city of Guadalajara in Mexico. Every day he drives to his ranch in his station wagon. Although he wears a baseball cap, on the seat alongside him sits his old wide-brimmed sombrero. "It's hard to get in and out of a car with a sombrero," don Pablo says with a chuckle. At the ranch he switches hats and rides out to inspect his prize cattle.

Horses and cattle were among the animals that the Spanish brought to the New World. In Mexico the settlers built *haciendas* to raise cattle. The ranchers were called *hacendados,* and the horsemen that rounded up, roped, and branded the cattle were called *charros*. The origins of the modern charro's clothes can be seen in the dress of the early hacendados. Many times throughout Mexico's history, the charros rode to defend their country. The charro, with his sombrero, lariat, and horse, has become a symbol of Mexico's pride and patriotism.

When the morning's chores are finished, don Pablo and the ranch hands gather to rest. One of the boys begins to *florear*, which means to spin *la reata*—the lariat—to make flowers in the air. His older brother joins him on horseback.

Naturally don Pablo can't resist, and soon he, too, is nimbly jumping in and out of his spinning lariat.

"This is what we have always done to relax after a hard day's work," says don Pablo. "The riding and roping skills of the charro that were once needed to work cattle have become the national sport called *la charrería*."

La Charreada

The most exciting part of *la charrería* is the rodeo-like competition called *la charreada*. A sea of sombreros fills a *lienzo,* a stadium where the *charreada* takes place. Above the arena is the grandstand for the spectators, many of whom are dressed in traditional clothes. The *charreada* starts when the riders fill the arena to sing the national anthem.

Then the *suertes* begin. These are the events that will test the charros' horsemanship, roping skills—and bravery.

The first suerte is the *cala de caballo,* a test to show how well a charro handles his horse. Each rider gallops into the ring. He reins in his mount, and the horse folds its rear legs and skids to a stop. Next the charro spins his horse, first to the right and then the left. With the slightest tug on the reins, he walks his horse backward. The suerte ends with a salute to the judges, after which the charro gallops out of the arena.

Piales —the next suerte—means lassoing an animal. Mounted charros take turns trying to rope the hind legs of a galloping *yegua,* or wild mare. The object is not to trip the horse but to slow it down to a standstill. If the charro succeeds in getting the lasso under the *yegua*'s hooves, he winds the rope once around his saddle horn to slow the running horse. Smoke rises from the friction of the rope spinning round the pommel.

Cola means tail. *Coleada* was the traditional way a charro would control a frisky young bull on the open range. When a young bull ran away from the herd, the charro gave chase, grabbed its tail, and brought it down. If the bull strayed again, the charro did it again. Eventually the bull got the idea and stayed with the herd.

In the *charreada* the charro gallops alongside a running bull, grabs its tail, and wraps it around his right leg; then he spins the bull to the ground. Four hooves in the air means a perfect *coleada*!

Jineteada de toros means bull riding. A bull is put in a chute and a strap is placed around its chest. The charro drops down onto the bull's back and grabs the strap with both hands. Then the chute is opened. Bull and rider leap into the arena, where the angry bull bucks and kicks. The suerte ends when the charro is thrown or the bull tires and stops.

For the *terna* three charros work together. They have eight minutes to rope a bull, bring it down, and release it. The firs charro lassos the head or horns of the bull. The next charro lassos the bull's ind legs. With their ropes around the saddle horns, the two riders move aprt, toppling the bull. The third rider quickly dismounts to release the animal.

In the next suerte, *jineteada de yeguas,* a charro rides a bucking wild horse bareback. The charro holds on to a strap while the bucking horse whips him back and forth. When the horse calms down, the charro grabs the *yegua*'s ear, removes the strap, and nimbly slips to the ground.

A burst of music from a band of *mariachis* signals an intermission. It is time for the *escaramuzas*.

Women and girls perform an equestrian ballet called *escaramuza charra*. The women ride sidesaddle wearing sombreros and elegant full-skirted dresses. The audience is moved to cheer at the sight of the *escaramuzas* galloping into the arena, their horses' manes and their frilled dresses fluttering in the wind.

Then the charros return. In the *manganas* the charro must lasso a galloping *yegua* by the front legs to bring it down.

The charro begins to *florear*, jumping back and forth through the spinning loop until the horse gallops by. Then he deftly tosses the lasso toward the *yegua*'s hooves. If the loop catches the legs, he braces himself and stops the rope, bringing the horse down. One of his teammates quickly removes the rope and the *yegua* trots back into the corral. *Manganas* are also performed on horseback.

The final and
most dangerous
suerte of all is the
paso de muerte, the
"leap of death."
As three teammates
chase a wild horse
along the wall,
one charro brings
his horse along-
side. He gets up
on his knees,
leaps onto the
yegua, and grabs
its flowing mane.
The *yegua* bucks
and kicks to
throw the rider.
Holding on only
by the mane
and his legs, the
charro must ride
the horse until it
tires and he can
calmly hop off.

Becoming a Charro

Boys learn the ways of the charro from the men in their family. They also attend schools where they are taught by champion charros. Their school vacations are spent spinning lariats, riding horses and calves, and roping young bulls and each other. They also learn the values that are reflected in the Spanish word *caballero,* which means both horseman *and* gentleman.

Becoming a Charra

While the boys perfect their roping, the girls practice their riding. A team of *escaramuzas* rehearses in blue jeans for the next day's *charreada*. The girls sit high on the saddle. The right knee is hooked into a yolk at the front of the saddle while the left foot fits into a stirrup. The horses are trained to respond quickly to the reins, and they execute fast, nimble movements.

Tomorrow is a big day for everyone, but especially for one little *charra*. This will be her first performance in a *charreada*. It is *el día del charro*, the day that celebrates charros throughout Mexico.

El día del charro

As the early morning sun rises behind the steeples of the Church of Our Lady of Guadalupe, elegantly dressed charros and *escaramuzas* assemble at the entrance.

The men and women both wear sombreros. The boys and men sport big bow ties, and wear tight pants and boots with spurs. Some have on elaborately embroidered short jackets. Others use leather chaps.

The *charras* wear short jackets with long riding skirts. The bright, colorful frilled dresses of the *escaramuzas* are called *adelitas,* after a song about the women who fought alongside their men during the revolution.

The church bells mix with the jingle of spurs as columns of elegant charros and colorful *escaramuzas* enter the church for the mass. The sanctuary is ablaze with a warm glow from the many candles around the altar. Together the multitude celebrates its faith and traditions.

The mass concluded, the riders mount up. Their horses are equipped with beautifully decorated bridles, saddles, and stirrups. Some charros have silver decorations along the sides of their trousers. Many wear pistols to symbolize their role as warriors in Mexico's history.

The riders, charros and charras, young and old, move on to the boulevards of Guadalajara. The spectacle evokes waves and cheers from the people along the sidewalks. The long parade winds its way into the plaza in front of the Governor's Palace. From the balcony the governor and other dignitaries greet the charros.

Mariachis

Across the street, on an ornate bandstand in the middle of the plaza, *mariachis* dressed in charro outfits sing and play the traditional songs called *rancheras*. The charro suit is also worn to dance the *jarabe tapatío*, the traditional Mexican hat dance.

When the parade ends, the charros, *escaramuzas*, and spectators leave the plaza to go to the various *charreadas* that will take place around the city

The Children's Charreada

An afternoon children's *charreada* fills the grandstand of the *lienzo*. Each young charro gallops and slides his horse into the arena for the *cala de caballo*. The young charro spins his horse, walks it backward, and completes the suerte with a salute and a gallop out of the arena.

With the encouragement of the older charros, the youngsters take turns throwing their lariats in the *piales*. The boys bite their lips as they spin their ropes, waiting for the right moment to throw. There are many misses.

In the *coleada* the small boys are only required to grab the tail of the running young bull. But the older boys must knock the bull down, after which they gallop up to the grandstand and, with big grins, salute the crowd.

In the *jineteada de toros,* the bulls are smaller than those used in the adult *charreada,* but to a boy, the ride is just as bumpy.

Another bull is released from the chute and the roping team rides into action for the *terna*. First a young charro lassos the bull's head and holds it while his teammate flips the lariat beneath the bull's hind feet. The two riders pull the legs out from under the bull and down it goes.

Behind the arena gates, parents prepare their daughters for the *escaramuza*. As the last bull lopes out of the arena, music fills the *lienzo*. The gates swing open and the girls ride in.

The young charras gallop around the ring. The flurry of their dresses mixes with the dust raised by their horses. They divide into two lines that crisscross each other. The two lines then charge toward one another, each rider passing between two others. After a final canter around the arena, the girls spin and gallop away to the sound of music and applause.

The *charreada* continues with the boys' *manganas*. Because they are smaller than the men, the boys are allowed to stand closer to the wall. But that puts them nearer to the path of the thundering horses. They bravely hold their ground as their partners drive the *yegua* toward them.

One boy manages to get his rope around the front legs of the wild mare. Gritting his teeth, he lets out the rope as he leans back with all his weight. The spectators in the grandstand hold their breath—and the horse goes down.

Pandemonium breaks out in the *lienzo*. Yells and cheers fill the air. Hats, shoes, boots, and shawls rain down into the arena as the spectators pay tribute to the boy's skill and courage. The young charro, smiling broadly, walks around the arena tossing the articles back to their owners in the grandstand.

Now the *lienzo* becomes hushed as the *paso de muerte* begins. Parents and teammates look on anxiously as three riders chase a wild mare around the arena. A young bareback charro coaxes his horse alongside the galloping *yegua*. He draws his legs up until he is crouched on his knees. Sucking in his breath, he leaps— and disappears between the horses.

A gasp goes up from the crowd, and for a moment all is quiet as the boy lies motionless in the dirt. But then his head pops up and he rises to his knees. He's fine, just a bit shaken up. He dusts off the dirt and is soon up on his horse. The audience applauds his courage.

It is late. The afternoon's long shadows are creeping across the arena. The spectators rise to their feet to cheer the young charros as they line up to receive their prizes.

Another *charreada* has ended. But the men, women, and children of Mexico will ride again to celebrate their traditions, because to be a charro is to be a Mexican.

A Charro's Glossary

adelita (a-del-íta) —a traditional woman's costume, named for the song "Adelita"

caballero (ka-ba-yé-ro) —horseman, gentleman

caballo (ka-bá-yo) —horse

cala de caballo (ka-la de ka-bá-yo) —a test of horsemanship

charra (chá-rra) —expert horsewoman, cowgirl

charreada (chá-rre-a-da) —a riding competition

charro (chá-rro) —expert horseman, cowboy

charrería (cha-rre-reí-a) —a Mexican sport for charros

cola (kó-la) —tail

coleada (ko-le-á-da) —a takedown by the tail

coleadero (ko-le-a-dé-ro) —the event of bringing the bull to the ground by its tail

colear (ko-le-ár) —to bring down a bull by twisting its tail

don (don) —title of respect for a man

El día del charro (el dí-a del chá-rro) —the day for celebrating charros in Mexico

escaramuza (es-ka-ra-mú-sa) —a women's or girls' riding team

escaramuza charra (es-ka-ra-mú-sa chá-rra) —a young woman's equestrian ballet

florear (flo-re-ár) —to spin a lariat

hacendado (a-sen-dá-do) —land owner, rancher, farmer

hacienda (a-syén-da) —farm, ranch

jarabe tapatío (ha-ra-be ta-pa-tí-o) —traditional Mexican hat dance

jineteada de toros (hi-ne-te-á-da de to-ros) —a bull ride

jineteada de yeguas (hi-ne-te-á-da de yé-gwas) —to break-in wild mares

lienzo (lién-so) —a sports arena used for the *charrería*

mangana (man-gá-na) —an event in which a horse's forefeet are roped

mariachis (ma-ryá-chis) —popular Mexican musicians and singers

paso de muerte (pá-so de muér-te) —"leap of death"; an event at a *charrería*

piale (py-ale) —lassoing an animal

ranchera (rran-ché-ra) —traditional Mexican song

reata (rre-á-ta) —lariat, a rope with a running noose used to catch animals

sombrero (som-bré-ro) —wide-brimmed hat

suerte (swér-te) —an event in a competition

terna (tér-na) —a set of three, an event in a competition

yegua (yé-gwa) —wild mare